Stepping Stones at Camp Clementine

Story by Suzanne Barton
Illustrations by Ramona Bruno

Stepping Stones at Camp Clementine

Text: Suzanne Barton
Publishers: Tania Mazzeo and Eliza Webb
Series consultant: Amanda Sutera
Hands on Heads Consulting
Editor: Jess Mackay
Project editor: Annabel Smith
Designer: Jess Kelly
Project designer: Danielle Maccarone
Illustrations: Ramona Bruno
Production controller: Renee Tome

NovaStar

ISBN 978 0 17 033476 1

Cengage Learning Australia
Level 5, 80 Dorcas Street
Southbank VIC 3006 Australia
Phone: 1300 790 853
Email: aust.nelsonprimary@cengage.com

For learning solutions, visit **cengage.com.au**

Printed in China by 1010 Printing International Ltd
1 2 3 4 5 6 7 29 28 27 26 25

Nelson acknowledges the Traditional Owners and Custodians of the lands of all First Nations Peoples. We pay respect to Elders past and present, and extend that respect to all First Nations Peoples today.

Contents

Chapter 1

Camp Clementine

"Nature walks, horse riding, toasting marshmallows under the stars – you'll love Camp Clementine," Gran said. "I went every year when I was your age."

Ava looked out the car window as the forest whizzed by. Gran had been called away on an important archaeology mission, so Ava had to go to a school-holiday camp for the first time. Ava had lived with Gran since she was little. Her school was right next door to the museum where Gran worked. They were always together – until now.

"I won't know anyone," Ava said. "Can I *please* come with you to the dig?"

"Brushing dirt off rocks is no way to spend the holidays. Camp will be much more fun," Gran said.

MAPS

"There's even a talent show at the end of the week," Gran continued. "I'll be back then to cheer you on."

"I don't have a talent," Ava said. "I'll just watch, I guess."

Gran was quiet for a moment. Then she said: "I wasn't going to tell you this, but I hid a present in the front pocket of your bag."

Ava opened the smallest zip of her backpack and felt around in the pocket. After a moment, her fingers closed around a small, smooth object. She held it up to the car window in the sunshine. It was Gran's river-stone necklace – a grey stone strung on an ancient leather cord.

"Are you sure?" Ava said. "You love this necklace."

"Not as much as I love you," Gran said with a grin. "My grandmother found that necklace among the ruins of a castle near our family's home town in Ireland. It has magical powers when the wearer is in need."

Yeah right, Ava thought. *I've heard this story a thousand times*. But she didn't want to hurt Gran's feelings.

"Thanks, Gran," Ava said, slipping the necklace back into her bag.

"You won't need any magic, though," Gran said. "All you need to do is be yourself. Who knows, maybe you'll make some 'forever friends'."

Ava's stomach lurched as Gran steered the car off the main road and down a dirt track. A few minutes later, they passed under a huge wooden arch. Etched into the top beam were the words "Welcome to Camp Clementine".

Gran parked the car next to a wide grassy area where lots of other children were getting dropped off. Ava got out of the car and hugged Gran tightly as a camp leader with a clipboard jogged towards them.

"Ava Ryan?" the camp leader said. "I'm Kym. And you're the last camper to arrive. Follow me!"

Chapter 2

Mulberry Cabin

Kym led Ava along a winding path, pointing out a little bridge over the river, horses in the stables, a hot-chocolate station outside the canteen and a big hall where the talent show would be held. Ava sighed. Everywhere she looked there were campers laughing and having fun together.

After a few minutes, the path curved into the forest where small log cabins were dotted among the trees. Tripping over the uneven ground, Ava followed Kym to a building with a dark-red door. Pop music was blaring from inside.

"This is where you'll sleep – Mulberry Cabin," Kym said loudly over the music.

Ava swallowed hard, thinking: *what if I don't fit in?*

Kym strode up the steps, swung the door open and pressed a button on a portable speaker to switch off the music. Ava followed and peeked around Kym. Inside the cabin she saw rows of bunk beds and three campers frozen mid-dance move.

"Campers, this is Ava. It's her first time at Camp Clementine," Kym said. "Please help her feel at home. Ava, grab an empty bunk and get settled. I'll see you later."

Ava waved shyly at the campers as Kym left. They were all dressed in jeans and oversized jackets. Ava suddenly felt self-conscious of her colourful dress and polka-dot leggings.

"I'm Maya," one of the campers said excitedly, tossing Ava's sleeping bag onto a bunk. "You can take this bed next to mine!"

"I'm Luis," another camper said with a grin. "I'm staying over in Kiwi Cabin."

"I'm Charlie," the final camper said. "And we're in the middle of rehearsal."

"We dance at the talent show every year," Maya said. "Charlie makes up our routines with all the latest, most popular moves. She's the best choreographer ever."

"We got second place last year. Hopefully this year we can finally win the trophy," Luis said, turning the music back on. "Check out our routine."

Ava sat on her bed as the trio performed a complicated dance.

They rocked, they rolled, they popped and locked. They were perfectly synchronised. Ava looked on in wonder. She knew she'd fall flat on her face if she tried those moves. She tripped over her feet just walking. Ava felt like she had no talent at all.

The dancers finished with a confident pose – their arms crossed and lips pouting.

"That was great," Ava said, clapping politely. "I've seen some of those moves online."

"Can you dance, Ava?" Maya asked with a beaming smile.

"Yeah, of course," Ava blurted out, desperate to fit in but instantly regretting her lie.

"You know," Luis said, turning to face everyone excitedly. "If we had four people, we could do that cool lift at the end of our routine."

Ava thought about her two left feet, and her mouth went dry.

"A move like that could help us win the talent show," Maya gushed. "What do you think, Charlie?"

"Maybe," Charlie said. "But Ava will have to audition."

Chapter 3

Jelly Legs

Please don't make me dance, Ava thought, feeling her cheeks flush. An audition would be the most embarrassing thing ever.

"Maybe later," Ava said, tipping the contents of her bag onto her bed. "I should unpack."

"Please, Ava. Just show us any dance steps you know, and we can teach you our routine later," Maya said. "It'll be fun."

Ava looked at Maya's encouraging face and wondered if the two of them could be friends. Then she saw the river-stone necklace among her pile of clothes.

Couldn't hurt, Ava thought.

As Ava slipped the necklace over her head, she felt a surprising wave of courage.

"Okay, I'll audition," Ava said, feeling stunned by her own words.

Ava crossed to the middle of the room as Charlie started the music. Then, to Ava's amazement, her feet began to move. And not only did they move but they performed the campers' dance routine perfectly. She rocked, she rolled, she popped and locked. With every step, Ava gained more confidence. Maya and Luis cheered, and even Charlie looked a little impressed.

Then something even more extraordinary happened. The river-stone necklace began to pulse with a warm light. Ava could see it softly glowing under her dress. Suddenly, Ava's arms were pinned to her sides and her feet felt like they were in fast forward. Ava saw Maya's eyes widen as her dance style changed into an Irish jig – her legs twisting and twirling expertly into speedy steps and giant leaps.

"Wow," Luis said. "What do you call that?"

Ava was too out of breath to answer as her feet kept moving, but she wondered whether she was remembering some of the Irish dancing steps that Gran had taught her when she was little.

A moment later, the music ended, but Ava continued dancing.

"You can stop now," Charlie said with a giggle.

But Ava couldn't stop. Her feet were moving so fast they had become a blur. In desperation, Ava ripped off the river-stone necklace and her legs immediately felt like jelly, sending her sprawling across the floor.

Ava scrambled to her feet – tears of humiliation pricking her eyes – and ran out of the cabin and through the trees. In the distance, she thought she heard Charlie laughing.

Chapter 4

Marshmallow Party

As the stars came out, Ava sat near a huge campfire toasting a marshmallow on a stick. She hadn't returned to Mulberry Cabin all afternoon. She'd sat with the horses and turned the river-stone necklace over and over, amazed to think that Gran could have been telling the truth about its powers all this time.

After the evening meal, all the campers had gathered around the fire for Camp Clementine's first-night-of-camp marshmallow party. Through the flames, Ava spotted Charlie stuffing marshmallows into her cheeks to do an impression of a squirrel for some younger kids.

Ava let her hair fall in front of her face and tried to be invisible. *These are the worst school holidays ever,* she thought.

Ava began counting the hours until Gran would come back to pick her up.

"Your marshmallow is on fire," a voice said.

Ava jolted upright and yanked her stick out of the flames. The outside of the marshmallow was burnt to a crisp, and the inside spilled onto the grass like molten lava.

"I like them ultra-toasted too," another voice said.

Ava looked around and saw Maya and Luis sitting next to her.

"Are you okay?" Maya asked. "We couldn't find you anywhere – we started to worry."

"I'm okay," Ava lied.

"How was your first day at camp?" Luis asked, sticking three new marshmallows into the fire.

"Pretty weird," Ava said. "Sorry about before."

"Nothing to be sorry about. We loved your dancing," Maya said enthusiastically. "You've got to join us in the talent show."

"Really?" Ava said. "I literally fell on the floor."

"Right up until then it was great." Luis chuckled, sandwiching marshmallows between crackers and chocolate. "Here, try this. It's called a s'more."

Still glowing from the compliment, Ava took the sticky treat and gobbled it up.

"Yum," she said.

"So where did you learn to dance like that, Ava?" Maya asked.

Ava struggled to find the words. How could she tell them that she was a terrible dancer … until she was bewitched by a magical stone?

"My gran taught me some Irish steps when I was younger," Ava said. "I guess they all came flooding back. I was wearing her necklace, after all."

Ava took the river-stone necklace out of her pocket and let it glint in the firelight.

"Gran said it's magic," Ava said. "I know it sounds crazy – I never believed her, but now I'm not so sure."

"Wait," Maya spluttered, spitting marshmallow goo into the cold night air. "I know that necklace. Follow me!"

Chapter 5

Secrets

Ava and Luis chased after Maya as she ran to the big hall. Inside, there were photos of campers from over the years stuck to a wall.

"There it is!" Maya said, pointing to a black-and-white picture.

Ava looked at the image – it was of a young girl in an Irish dancing outfit, holding a trophy. The river-stone was hanging around her neck. But there was something else familiar about the photo.

"That's my gran!" Ava exclaimed. "She came to Camp Clementine, too."

"Looks like you aren't the only brilliant Irish dancer in your family," Luis said. "That's the talent-show trophy she's holding."

Ava felt her face flush with pride at Luis's words. She looked closely at the photo on the wall and saw how happy Gran looked.

Then she felt a little sad. Gran had always tried to share her love for Irish music and dancing with Ava, taking her to special classes and community parties called *céilís*. Ava had always felt too shy and uncoordinated to join in, but the river-stone necklace had made her feel full of joy and confidence.

Maya flopped into a nearby chair and sighed. “Can I tell you a secret?” she said, not pausing for a reply. “I wish I could dance Irish steps like that. I’m sick of the dance routines we do at the talent show every year.”

"Same," Luis said. "I don't want to do the exact same steps everyone else is doing online. *Boring*. My family is Spanish, and we love dancing flamenco."

Luis puffed out his chest and began to stride around the hall, clapping his hands, then arching his arms above his head. He grabbed a flower out of a vase, held it between his teeth and stomped his feet faster and faster.

Maya giggled and began drumming on the table. “I want to dance bhangra, just like in a Bollywood movie,” she said. “I once saw one being filmed when I was visiting my aunties in India.”

Ava watched as Maya leapt to her feet and began to perform energetic dance moves – jumping from side to side, pumping her arms and waving her scarf in the air.

“That’s awesome!” Ava said, as Maya and Luis continued their Spanish and Indian dance routines around the hall. “These kinds of dances would definitely win the talent show.”

Maya and Luis finished their dances with a flourish, then looked at each other sadly.

"I don't think Charlie will want to change our dance," Luis said.

"Yeah," Maya said. "Charlie only wants to do the latest moves she sees online. We have to be exactly the same, like robots. I don't want to be a robot – we should dance what's in our hearts."

A sudden sob echoed around the hall. Everyone whirled around and saw Charlie standing in the doorway.

“Do whatever you want at the talent show,” Charlie spat. “I quit!”

“Charlie, we didn’t mean–” Maya started to plead, but it was too late. Charlie had run away into the darkness.

“She’s heading towards the river,” Ava said from the doorway.

Luis opened a supply cupboard and grabbed some big torches.

“Let’s go,” he said.

Chapter 6

Spotlight

Ava crept through the trees near the river, leaves crunching under her feet. Maya and Luis were just ahead of her, scanning the darkness with their torches.

"Charlie! Charlie!" Maya called.

Ava listened closely – the wind was whistling through the branches and the river was lapping up against the rocks. And then there was a tiny sniffle.

"Found her," Luis shouted, pointing his torch up into the branches of a tree.

Ava looked up and saw a treehouse among the leaves. Charlie was peering down at them, her cheeks glistening with tears.

"We're coming up," Maya said.

Maya and Luis raced up the wooden ladder and Ava followed timidly.

They all gathered around Charlie, and Ava tried to avoid Charlie's eyes.

It's my fault everyone is arguing, Ava thought.

"Shouldn't you three be practising your new dance?" Charlie sneered.

“It wouldn’t be the same without you, Charlie,” Maya said.

“Yeah, please don’t quit the group,” Luis said. “We can still do your routine – it’s really cool. We were just playing around with the dances our families do.”

"My family doesn't have a special cultural dance ... unless you count my dad's embarrassing kitchen dancing," Charlie said.

Everyone was quiet for a moment, then Ava had an idea. She pulled the river-stone necklace out of her pocket and put it around Charlie's neck.

"I know it sounds weird but, when I was stuck and sad, this necklace helped me dance what was in my heart," Ava said.

"As if," Charlie scoffed, but then she gasped. The necklace had started to glow.

Without saying a word, Charlie climbed down the ladder to a grassy circle at the foot of the tree. Everyone shone their torches down, putting Charlie in the spotlight. And then – to the rhythms of crickets, wind and rushing water – Charlie started to dance.

She twirled in pirouettes around the pool of light. Then she switched from ballet to tap dancing, her arms and legs moving like windmills in hypersonic speed. Then, she dropped to the ground and spun in a ball like a breakdancer.

Ava, Luis and Maya cheered as Charlie whipped up a mini tornado of leaves. But then the necklace fell off and Charlie spun to a stop.

"It's no use," Charlie said, lying sprawled like a starfish. "My styles are all mixed up. I don't have a 'heart dance' like you all do."

Just then, a voice shouted from the darkness.

"*There* you all are," Kym said. "Back to your cabins. It's time for lights out!"

Ava scooped up the necklace and followed the others back through the trees.

Chapter 7

New Steps

The next morning, Ava was lying awake listening to Maya and Charlie snore in perfect harmony when the cabin door flew open. The girls jolted awake and saw Luis grinning in the doorway.

"I've got big news," he said.

"Wherfs goffung ern?" Maya mumbled. Then she spat out her night guard and repeated: "What's going on?"

"I just heard that my grandfather is coming to visit from Spain, and he's going to watch the talent show," Luis said. "I have to dance flamenco! It would make my abuelo so happy."

"I think you should, Luis," Maya said. "I'd love to dance bhangra for my parents, too. And Ava, I bet your gran would be so proud to see your Irish steps."

Everyone turned hesitantly to Charlie, who was still rolled up in her blanket like a burrito.

"You three do your dances," Charlie said, rolling away to face the wall. "I'll just watch."

"No way," Maya said. "We're a team. We need you."

No one knew what to say for a minute, then Ava had an idea.

"Who says we each have to dance in one particular way?" Ava said. "How about we make up a new group routine that celebrates *all* the styles we love?"

"Perfect!" Luis said. "But that sounds tricky. We'd need the *best choreographer ever.*"

Luis gave Charlie a playful nudge and she rolled back towards them with a grin.

For the rest of the week, Ava, Charlie, Maya and Luis worked hard on the new dance routine.

Kym helped them edit together music from all over the world. The sewing club helped them make colourful costumes. And Charlie worked hardest of all – learning steps from Ireland, India and Spain and combining them with a medley of her favourite modern moves into one spectacular super-dance.

As Ava practised the routine, the river-stone necklace glowed softly inside her hoodie, helping her keep up with the moves.

On the night before the talent show, the dancers sat along the back deck of Mulberry Cabin with mugs of hot chocolate, looking out into the misty forest. Ava smiled to herself as the campers laughed and joked around her. She felt like she'd made three "forever friends".

It's all thanks to Gran's necklace, Ava thought. She reached up to feel the river-stone around her neck – but it was gone.

"I've lost my necklace!" Ava shrieked, leaping to her feet.

"It's okay, we'll find it," Maya said, searching the ground.

"Let's look tomorrow when it's light," Charlie said with a yawn. "I'm exhausted."

"I need it for the concert," Ava said.

"We don't need anything but our amazing moves, costumes and music," Luis said. "That trophy is ours."

But Ava wasn't so sure.

Without the necklace, I'll ruin everything, she thought.

Chapter 8

Showtime

The next morning, the necklace was still nowhere to be seen. Ava's nerves grew as she had breakfast and helped decorate the hall. Then it was time to get ready for the talent show. Sitting backstage, the butterflies in her stomach felt like they were doing an Irish dance of their own.

"Don't worry," Maya said, applying sparkly eyeshadow. "You'll be fantastic."

"You don't understand," Ava whispered. "Without the necklace, I can't dance at all."

Maya looked at Ava thoughtfully.

"It's okay, I'll be right there next to you," she said.

"Quiet backstage," Kym whispered. "It's showtime!"

For the next half an hour, Ava watched from backstage as a series of campers took to the stage. There was a beatboxer, a magician, and a very small child with a very large accordion. Peering through a crack in the curtains, Ava winced as she saw Gran sitting in the front row.

I'll never win a trophy like Gran did, Ava thought. *Everyone is going to laugh at me.*

"You're next," Kym whispered to Ava. "But where did the rest of your group go?"

Ava looked around in panic and breathed a sigh of relief when she saw Maya, Charlie and Luis running up to her – just in time. To Ava's surprise, Luis was holding the river-stone necklace.

"Look what we found," Luis whispered, slipping the necklace over Ava's head.

Ava squealed and thanked them all with a group hug. Finally feeling brave, Ava led the way onto the stage as their music started.

The dance began with energetic solos. Maya's parents beamed as she danced liked a Bollywood star. Luis's abuelo shouted encouragement in Spanish as his grandson stomped rhythmic flamenco steps. And Charlie's brothers whooped as she popped, locked and twirled across the stage.

Then Ava ran forward to perform the Irish dancing steps. Her feet felt like they were flying. When Ava looked down into the audience, she saw her gran's eyes shining with happy tears.

To finish their routine, all four dancers came together to showcase a medley of moves from around the world. As the music swelled, families began dancing in the aisles.

When the dancers struck their final pose, the audience roared with applause.

After the show, Ava left Gran chatting with Luis's abuelo and sat on the jetty with Maya, Luis and Charlie. They held up their trophy proudly and took a group selfie.

"Best day ever," Ava said. "It's weird though – my necklace isn't glowing any more."

Ava noticed the others look at each other strangely as Kym jogged up to them.

"I heard you were missing some jewellery, Ava. Someone just handed this in to lost property," Kym said, holding up *another* river-stone necklace.

Ava compared the two necklaces in confusion.

"We've got a confession to make," Maya said softly. "We found a stone from the river and pretended it was your necklace."

Ava felt a moment of shock – she'd danced all by herself, with no magical help. But somehow, she'd still felt Gran's encouragement flowing through her feet.

"Those moves were in you all along," Charlie said. "I guess the necklace just made you feel confident."

"You aren't angry with us, are you?" Luis said.

Ava looked at her new friends' hopeful faces and smiled.

"Of course not," she said. "I think I want to come back to Camp Clementine every year."